Greater Thoughts

The Un-Trapped Mind

Robert C. Collins Sr.

THE
WRITER'S
GAME

The Writers Game

Greater Thoughts

The Un-Trapped Mind

Robert C. Collins Sr.

THE
WRITER'S
GAME

The Writers Game

"Watch your thoughts; they become words. Watch your words; they become actions. Watch your actions; they become habits. Watch your habits; they become character. Watch your character; it becomes your destiny."

- Lao Tzu

The Writers Game

8936 Northpointe Executive Park Drive, Ste 260,

Huntersville, NC 28078

info@thewritersgame.com

GREATER THOUGHTS

www.thewritersgame.com

ISBN: 979-8-9877109-6-8

eBook ISBN: 979-8-9877109-7-5

Printed in The United States of America

A Message To You,

This book is dedicated to you, the seeker of self-awareness and the conscious creator of your own reality. Within these pages, I invite you on a transformative journey—a journey that begins within your mind.

Here, you will discover the profound influence your thoughts hold over your life. Together, we will navigate the intricacies of your inner landscape, empowering you to correct unhelpful thoughts and nurture those that support your aspirations.

As you engage with the exercises and reflections within, remember that change takes time and effort. Embrace the opportunity to reshape your thoughts, casting aside self-doubt and fear, and cultivating a mindset that aligns with your highest vision.

You hold the key to unlocking extraordinary potential. With every thought, you have the power to recreate your reality. Embrace this book as a guide on your journey of self-discovery, and may it inspire you to manifest a life filled with love, purpose, joy, and authenticity.

With gratitude and belief in your limitless potential,

Robert C. Collins Sr.

Contents

Greater Thoughts

"Cultivating and enhancing your thoughts is like tending to a garden of possibilities. It is within the fertile soil of your mind that seeds of innovation, understanding, and personal growth take root and flourish. Nourish your thoughts with curiosity, nurture them with knowledge, and watch as they bloom into the extraordinary ideas that shape your world."

In embarking upon this remarkable expedition into uncharted territories of the mind, there are vital revelations that I am eager to share with you. These insights hold the key to unlocking a profound understanding of how the mind truly operates.

At the very core of this understanding lies the concept of energy—the life force that powers your mind and influences your entire being. It is through this energy that your inherent power manifests in diverse and fascinating ways. Among the many facets to explore, there is one particular aspect that warrants your utmost attention: the power of repetition and the remarkable process of cell reproduction.

Picture this: within the intricate recesses of your mind, cells multiply, perpetuating the very thoughts and ideas you nourish. When you embrace a positive or negative thought, these remarkable cells are generated within the profound confines of your brain's hypothalamus region.

Here's the crux of the matter: when you introduce a positive thought into your mind, a cascade of cells associated with that uplifting energy spring to life. These newly reproduced cells persist until a subsequent notion takes their place. However, consider the influences that have shaped many of us during our formative years. We have been burdened with limitations imposed upon us, with people declaring that certain aspirations lie beyond our grasp.

Let it be known that these constraints do not define you. They are products of the environment in which you grew, infused into your very being. Consequently, a multitude of negative thoughts have permeated your consciousness, permeating through those resilient cells. The objective, then, for the next 90 days is to redefine the patterns of your thinking, to empower your cells in generating unwavering streams of positivity.

By nurturing a mindset that embraces positivity, you shall

reside within a realm teeming with optimism. The energy emanating from this newfound positivity will fuel and sustain your unwavering momentum. Over the course of these transformative 90 days, you will embark upon a daily ritual—a deliberate focus on ensuring your cells consistently generate positive energy. In doing so, you shall chart a fresh trajectory for your life, brimming with boundless possibilities.

Chapter One

The Power Within: Unveiling The Influence of Your Thoughts

"Your thoughts have the power to shape your reality and influence your journey. Choose them wisely, for they can either be the chains that bind you or the wings that set you free."

First and foremost, I express my gratitude to you, the reader, for investing your time in this journey. The purpose of this book, titled "Greater Thoughts," is to guide you from your current thought process to a more empowering and fruitful mindset in the future. Although the process may require effort and dedication, I assure you that it will be well worth it.

Our journey begins with developing a deeper understanding of your own thoughts and becoming more conscious of them. It is essential to recognize the thoughts that pass through your mind, whether they arise upon waking up, during the day, or even while daydreaming. Some thoughts may come and go without much impact, while others may trigger reactive behaviors without thoughtful consideration. These reactive thoughts do not serve your best interests or align with the person you truly want to be. It is crucial to remove these negative patterns and avoid speaking or acting in ways that contradict your desired self-image.

In this book, I will assist you in taking your time to read and engage with the activities provided. Progress will be made day by day, as everything in life starts with one moment at a time. It is important to remember that dwelling on the past does not serve your future. Your past experiences have shaped your present, but now the focus, is on embracing a new path forward.

Before we delve into the practice of being conscious of your thoughts and engaging in positive activities, such as affirmations or motivational quotes, let's take a moment to understand how thoughts work. Imagine yourself at work, and upon seeing your manager enter the room, a chain of thoughts begins to unfold. Perhaps you worry that they will approach you, reflecting on a challenging day you had previously. The chain continues as you contemplate the fate of a co-worker who faced a similar situation and got fired. Suddenly, you find yourself consumed by thoughts of impending doom, wondering how long it will be before you receive notice of termination and how it will impact your financial stability and responsibilities.

However, reality paints a different picture. The manager's arrival at work may have been unrelated to your performance, and your thoughts have taken an unproductive and fearful turn. This example illustrates how our thoughts can lead us astray if left unchecked. Let me explain further how the hypothalamus, a part of your brain, plays a role in this process and how we can utilize it to our advantage.

The hypothalamus is a vital component of the central nervous system, responsible for various functions, including emotions, behaviors, and health. It influences how you feel, react, and move based on your thoughts, whether they are positive, negative, or neutral. Every thought triggers a corresponding reaction within your body. These reactions can manifest as inaction, further contemplation, or even physical movement. Furthermore, thoughts impact the secretion of hormones, which play a significant role in your overall well-being.

When you have a thought, it forms a chain of cells that multiply and become larger molecules in the hypothalamus. These molecules, called peptides, are continually recreated and reproduce based on their original source. Whether positive, neutral, or negative, these thoughts shape the peptides and, subsequently, our experiences and behaviors. As a child, you encounter a spectrum of words that shape your self-perception, ranging from empowering affirmations like "you can achieve anything with determination" and "you're exceptionally intelligent" to discouraging statements such as "you won't amount to anything" or comparisons to someone who is not held in high regard. These instances represent just a few examples of how your self-image begins to form early in life.

In this chapter, our focus is on cultivating awareness of your thoughts. To begin this process, we will spend the first 30 days practicing consciousness. Just as you would prepare for a workout at the gym, taking time to think about your goals and set intentions, we will lay the foundation for our mental workout. Each day, we will incorporate a quote or affirmation to guide your consciousness. The goal is to reach a point where negative thoughts are intercepted and replaced with positive ones, realigning you with your desired path in life. To counteract negative thoughts or limiting beliefs, the aim is to regularly recite positive quotes that resonate with you, thereby fostering a constructive mindset throughout your days.

Each day, you will have space to journal your experiences, and I have also provided additional guidance in the form of an activity. This exercise, will likely open your eyes to the thoughts that have been running through your mind, holding you back or leading you astray. I encourage you to embrace this opportunity for growth and transformation. By picking up this book, you have embarked on a journey that will motivate and inspire you, leading to a new outlook on life. At the end of this journey, you will not only witness personal change but also attribute the glory to a higher power.

This is not solely about self-help or self-love; it transcends that realm. It's about love in its purest form, and by the end, you will emerge as a better version of yourself. Get ready for an exciting transformation. Continue reading, and let's embark on this journey together.

Day 1

Sprint to your positive thoughts & Flee from your negative State of mind.

Weekly Guided Scripture

"Do not conform to the pattern of this world, but be transformed by the renewing of your mind. Then you will be able to test and approve what God's will is—his good, pleasing and perfect will."- **Romans 12:2 NIV**

Today's Activity:

Spend the day mindfully observing your thoughts without judgment. Notice any recurring patterns or themes.

_____

_____

_____

_____

_____

_____

_____

_____

_____

Daily Reflection:

Use the page below to write your feelings or reflections from the chapter or take this time to write out your action plan to begin Creating Greater Thoughts.

Day 2
Be Positive, It costs nothing!

Weekly Guided Scripture
"Do not conform to the pattern of this world, but be transformed by the renewing of your mind. Then you will be able to test and approve what God's will is—his good, pleasing and perfect will."- **Romans 12:2 NIV**

Today's Activity:
Write a list of 3 or more things that brings you joy and reflect on them when you find your thoughts not serving you. Speak them aloud.

_____

_____

_____

_____

_____

_____

_____

_____

_____

_____

Daily Reflection:

Use the page below to write your feelings or reflections from the chapter or take this time to write out your action plan to begin Creating Greater Thoughts.

Day 3

Challenge yourself, believe that your reality goes beyond what you see. Make your thoughts, Reality

Weekly Guided Scripture

"Do not conform to the pattern of this world, but be transformed by the renewing of your mind. Then you will be able to test and approve what God's will is—his good, pleasing and perfect will."- **Romans 12:2 NIV**

Today's Activity:

Start a gratitude journal. In this journal daily write 3 things that you are grateful for, even if it's not seen yet. Write to your future self.

_____

_____

_____

_____

_____

_____

_____

_____

_____

Daily Reflection:

Use the page below to write your feelings or reflections from the chapter or take this time to write out your action plan to begin Creating Greater Thoughts.

Day 4
When you don't know, Just listen to the Lord!

Weekly Guided Scripture

"Do not conform to the pattern of this world, but be transformed by the renewing of your mind. Then you will be able to test and approve what God's will is—his good, pleasing and perfect will."- **Romans 12:2 NIV**

Today's Activity:

Engage in a guided visualization exercise. Visualize yourself achieving a goal or living your ideal life. Notice the emotions and thoughts that arise during this practice.

_____

_____

_____

_____

_____

_____

_____

_____

_____

Daily Reflection:

Use the page below to write your feelings or reflections from the chapter or take this time to write out your action plan to begin Creating Greater Thoughts.

Day 5

Make their mental limitations be the floor to your life's expectations. Rise above!

Weekly Guided Scripture

"Do not conform to the pattern of this world, but be transformed by the renewing of your mind. Then you will be able to test and approve what God's will is—his good, pleasing and perfect will."- **Romans 12:2 NIV**

Today's Activity:

Pay close attention to your thoughts today. Whenever you catch yourself thinking negatively, consciously replace it with a positive thought. Remember there are limitless possibilities.

_____

_____

_____

_____

_____

_____

_____

_____

_____

Daily Reflection:

Use the page below to write your feelings or reflections from the chapter or take this time to write out your action plan to begin Creating Greater Thoughts.

Day 6

Believe when, No one else Does! Trust in yourself, When everyone else gives up! Live and Love, When others speak Death and Hate!

Weekly Guided Scripture

"Do not conform to the pattern of this world, but be transformed by the renewing of your mind. Then you will be able to test and approve what God's will is—his good, pleasing and perfect will."- **Romans 12:2 NIV**

Today's Activity:

Spend the day in positive environments and with uplifting people. Observe how these external influences impact your thoughts and overall mindset.

_____

_____

_____

_____

_____

_____

_____

_____

_____

Daily Reflection:

Use the page below to write your feelings or reflections from the chapter or take this time to write out your action plan to begin Creating Greater Thoughts.

Day 7

To be open minded, Requires the removal of fear and ego!

First, one has to realize their mind is trapped.

Weekly Guided Scripture

"Do not conform to the pattern of this world, but be transformed by the renewing of your mind. Then you will be able to test and approve what God's will is—his good, pleasing and perfect will."- **Romans 12:2 NIV**

Today's Activity:

Practice meditating for five minutes remembering F.E.A. R. False Evidence Appearing Real & E.G.O. Edging God out, Let go and take notice to how this calms the mind.

_____

_____

_____

_____

_____

_____

_____

_____

_____

Daily Reflection:

Use the page below to write your feelings or reflections from the chapter or take this time to write out your action plan to begin Creating Greater Thoughts.

Day 8

Alive, So I am grateful! I show gratitude by my actions, not just by my words!

Weekly Guided Scripture

"for he is the kind of person who is always thinking about the cost
"Eat and drink," he says to you, but his heart is not with you."
- Proverbs 23:7 KJV

Today's Activity:

Engage in physical activity such as pilates or exercise. Observe how the movement of your body affects your thoughts and mental well-being.

Daily Reflection:

Use the page below to write your feelings or reflections from the chapter or take this time to write out your action plan to begin Creating Greater Thoughts.

Day 9
Feel good! God gave us victory!

Weekly Guided Scripture

"for he is the kind of person who is always thinking about the cost

"Eat and drink," he says to you, but his heart is not with you."

- Proverbs 23:7 KJV

Today's Activity:

Identify a limiting belief you hold about yourself. Dissect it, challenge it, and reframe it with a victorious affirmation. Observe the shift in your mindset.

_____

_____

_____

_____

_____

_____

_____

_____

_____

Daily Reflection:

Use the page below to write your feelings or reflections from the chapter or take this time to write out your action plan to begin Creating Greater Thoughts.

Day 10

Misery loves company, so have no fear when speaking prosperity into your own life! Opposites attract only in magnets!

Weekly Guided Scripture

"for he is the kind of person who is always thinking about the cost
"Eat and drink," he says to you, but his heart is not with you."
- Proverbs 23:7 KJV

Today's Activity:

Perform random acts of kindness throughout the day. Notice the positive impact it has on your thoughts and emotions.

_____

_____

_____

_____

_____

_____

_____

_____

_____

_____

Daily Reflection:

Use the page below to write your feelings or reflections from the chapter or take this time to write out your action plan to begin Creating Greater Thoughts.

Day 11

Y? believe in God! But not believe in yourself? When God's
Spirit lives within you!

Weekly Guided Scripture

*"for he is the kind of person who is always thinking about the
cost*
"Eat and drink," he says to you, but his heart is not with you."
- Proverbs 23:7 KJV

Today's Activity:

Write something that you've been believing God for but
haven't yet had the confidence to speak. Think about how it
makes you feel to have it through visualization.

_____

_____

_____

_____

_____

_____

_____

_____

_____

Daily Reflection:

Use the page below to write your feelings or reflections from the chapter or take this time to write out your action plan to begin Creating Greater Thoughts.

Day 12

Attack the things you are most afraid of! Conquering your fears requires you to do something! Have faith!

Weekly Guided Scripture

"for he is the kind of person who is always thinking about the cost
"Eat and drink," he says to you, but his heart is not with you."
- Proverbs 23:7 KJV

Today's Activity:

Do one thing today that brings you closer to conquering a goal you have been holding on to. Write how completing that one thing made you feel.

_____

_____

_____

_____

_____

_____

_____

_____

_____

Daily Reflection:

Use the page below to write your feelings or reflections from the chapter or take this time to write out your action plan to begin Creating Greater Thoughts.

Day 13

God had a thought and the Earth was created! Man had a thought and planes and submarines were created! What are you thinking?

Weekly Guided Scripture

"for he is the kind of person who is always thinking about the cost
"Eat and drink," he says to you, but his heart is not with you. "
- Proverbs 23:7 KJV

Today's Activity:

Take a break from social media for the day. Pay attention to how it affects your thoughts and mental clarity.

_____

_____

_____

_____

_____

_____

_____

_____

_____

Daily Reflection:

Use the page below to write your feelings or reflections from the chapter or take this time to write out your action plan to begin Creating Greater Thoughts.

Day 14

Life is full of joy and abundance! If you focus on the lows and the things you can't control, life will end & you will have missed it!

Weekly Guided Scripture

"for he is the kind of person who is always thinking about the cost
"Eat and drink," he says to you, but his heart is not with you."
- **Proverbs 23:7 KJV**

Today's Activity:

Practice mindful eating by savoring each bite and being fully present during meals. Observe how this conscious act impacts your thoughts and relationship with food.

_____

_____

_____

_____

_____

_____

_____

_____

_____

Daily Reflection:

Use the page below to write your feelings or reflections from the chapter or take this time to write out your action plan to begin Creating Greater Thoughts.

Day 15

Challenge! Believe that you have conquered, the subpar thoughts in your mind holding you complacent!

Weekly Guided Scripture

"The tongue has the power of life and death, and those who love it will eat its fruit." - **Proverbs 18:21 NIV**

Today's Activity:

Set aside time for self-reflection. Journal about your journey so far and the shifts you have noticed in your thought patterns.

_____

_____

_____

_____

_____

_____

_____

_____

_____

Daily Reflection:

Use the page below to write your feelings or reflections from the chapter or take this time to write out your action plan to begin Creating Greater Thoughts.

Day 16

All great structures have protection, so likewise, be a security guard to your thoughts.

Weekly Guided Scripture

"The tongue has the power of life and death, and those who love it will eat its fruit." - **Proverbs 18:21 NIV**

Today's Activity:

Identify any negative influences in your environment, such as toxic relationships or draining activities. Take steps to remove or minimize these influences.

_____

_____

_____

_____

_____

_____

_____

_____

_____

Daily Reflection:

Use the page below to write your feelings or reflections from the chapter or take this time to write out your action plan to begin Creating Greater Thoughts.

Day 17

Allow yourself to be uncomfortable, GROWTH requires
you to expand your comfort zone.

Weekly Guided Scripture

*"The tongue has the power of life and death, and those who love
it will eat its fruit."* - **Proverbs 18:21 NIV**

Today's Activity:

Try something today that you have been running from
because it was out of your comfort zone. Write how it feels
to overcome that anxiety.

_____

_____

_____

_____

_____

_____

_____

_____

_____

Daily Reflection:

Use the page below to write your feelings or reflections from the chapter or take this time to write out your action plan to begin Creating Greater Thoughts.

Day 18

I am making the choice to misplace the trauma that displaces my emotion.

Weekly Guided Scripture

"The tongue has the power of life and death, and those who love it will eat its fruit." - **Proverbs 18:21 NIV**

Today's Activity:

Speak – I allow myself to take old trauma and remove it from my current being. Allow it to be moved to an old experience in your life and no longer carry the trauma. Write how it makes you feel.

Daily Reflection:

Use the page below to write your feelings or reflections from the chapter or take this time to write out your action plan to begin Creating Greater Thoughts.

Day 19

Where has your mind taken you? If it's to positivity, keep the good energy flowing! If not, "you" change your thoughts!

Weekly Guided Scripture

"The tongue has the power of life and death, and those who love it will eat its fruit." - **Proverbs 18:21 NIV**

Today's Activity:

Read an inspirational book or article. Reflect on the empowering thoughts and ideas it introduces to your mind.

_____

_____

_____

_____

_____

_____

_____

_____

_____

Daily Reflection:

Use the page below to write your feelings or reflections from the chapter or take this time to write out your action plan to begin Creating Greater Thoughts.

Day 20

I am my thoughts! There is no other moment, there is only right now!

Weekly Guided Scripture

"The tongue has the power of life and death, and those who love it will eat its fruit." - **Proverbs 18:21 NIV**

Today's Activity:

Stop! take 6 minutes right now! Do something that you have been putting off for far to long. If you can't finish now it's okay. You just accomplished starting.

_____

_____

_____

_____

_____

_____

_____

_____

_____

Daily Reflection:

Use the page below to write your feelings or reflections from the chapter or take this time to write out your action plan to begin Creating Greater Thoughts.

Day 21

Whether it's Lack or Abundance. The thoughts you focus on most are what you yield, Choose Abundance!

Weekly Guided Scripture

"The tongue has the power of life and death, and those who love it will eat its fruit." - **Proverbs 18:21 NIV**

Today's Activity:

Consciously seek out positive news, stories, or experiences throughout the day. Notice how this focus on optimism influences your thoughts and outlook.

_____

_____

_____

_____

_____

_____

_____

_____

_____

Daily Reflection:

Use the page below to write your feelings or reflections from the chapter or take this time to write out your action plan to begin Creating Greater Thoughts.

Day 22

Today I rise above all adversity! My mind is renewed! I refuse to allow negativity into my thoughts! I am created from love!

Weekly Guided Scripture

"Now faith is confidence in what we hope for and assurance about what we do not see." - **Hebrews 11:1**

Today's Activity:

Clear out the negative social media accounts from your feed today. Share your thoughts on the experience of eliminating them.

_____

_____

_____

_____

_____

_____

_____

_____

_____

_____

Daily Reflection:

Use the page below to write your feelings or reflections from the chapter or take this time to write out your action plan to begin Creating Greater Thoughts.

Day 23

Desires invoke thoughts, thoughts invoke emotions, emotions invoke work, work towards your desires. Bring your dreams into reality!

Weekly Guided Scripture

"Now faith is confidence in what we hope for and assurance about what we do not see." - **Hebrews 11:1**

Today's Activity:

Spend time in nature, immersing yourself in its beauty. Observe how being in nature affects your thoughts and overall well-being.

_____

_____

_____

_____

_____

_____

_____

_____

_____

Daily Reflection:

Use the page below to write your feelings or reflections from the chapter or take this time to write out your action plan to begin Creating Greater Thoughts.

Day 24

Your mind. Is your most powerful tool! Do you positively or negatively charge it?

Weekly Guided Scripture

"Now faith is confidence in what we hope for and assurance about what we do not see." - **Hebrews 11:1**

Today's Activity:

Practice self-compassion by speaking kindly to yourself and acknowledging your worth. Observe the impact on your thoughts and self-perception.

_____

_____

_____

_____

_____

_____

_____

_____

_____

Daily Reflection:

Use the page below to write your feelings or reflections from the chapter or take this time to write out your action plan to begin Creating Greater Thoughts.

Day 25

My smiles during tough times exist, cause I know on the other side is great pleasure!

Weekly Guided Scripture

"Now faith is confidence in what we hope for and assurance about what we do not see." - **Hebrews 11:1**

Today's Activity:

Consciously limit your useless screen time and engage in mindful technology use. Observe how this intentional approach affects your thoughts and overall well-being.

_____

_____

_____

_____

_____

_____

_____

_____

_____

Daily Reflection:

Use the page below to write your feelings or reflections from the chapter or take this time to write out your action plan to begin Creating Greater Thoughts.

Day 26

The brightest shining light in the room! I won, before "IT" even started! I am Victorious!

Weekly Guided Scripture

"Now faith is confidence in what we hope for and assurance about what we do not see." - **Hebrews 11:1**

Today's Activity:

Engage in a visualization exercise that focuses on your goals and aspirations. Pay attention to the thoughts and emotions that arise during this practice.

_____

_____

_____

_____

_____

_____

_____

_____

_____

Daily Reflection:

Use the page below to write your feelings or reflections from the chapter or take this time to write out your action plan to begin Creating Greater Thoughts.

Day 27

The change you want to see in the world begins with making a change within yourself.

Weekly Guided Scripture

"Now faith is confidence in what we hope for and assurance about what we do not see." - **Hebrews 11:1**

Today's Activity:

Throughout the day, practice making decisions consciously and intentionally. Observe how this approach influences your thoughts and outcomes.

_____

_____

_____

_____

_____

_____

_____

_____

_____

Daily Reflection:

Use the page below to write your feelings or reflections from the chapter or take this time to write out your action plan to begin Creating Greater Thoughts.

Day 28

My positive thoughts will create and attract more positive energy so my Attitude is gratitude.

Weekly Guided Scripture

"Now faith is confidence in what we hope for and assurance about what we do not see." - **Hebrews 11:1**

Today's Activity:

Reflect on the progress you have made during these 28 days. Celebrate the positive shifts in your thoughts and mindset.

_____

_____

_____

_____

_____

_____

_____

_____

_____

_____

Daily Reflection:

Use the page below to write your feelings or reflections from the chapter or take this time to write out your action plan to begin Creating Greater Thoughts.

Day 29

Nothing is guaranteed except right now! You are not living later, you are living now! Enjoy this moment!

Weekly Guided Scripture

"Now faith is confidence in what we hope for and assurance about what we do not see." - **Hebrews 11:1**

Today's Activity:

Be Intentional! 3 times today stop for 60 seconds and just enjoy the moment.

_____

_____

_____

_____

_____

_____

_____

Daily Reflection:

Use the page below to write your feelings or reflections from the chapter or take this time to write out your action plan to begin Creating Greater Thoughts.

Day 30

Since I am connected to infinite power, I shall not complain.

Weekly Guided Scripture

"Now faith is confidence in what we hope for and assurance about what we do not see." - **Hebrews 11:1**

Today's Activity:

Create a list of things that you have overcome since starting this journey to Greater Thoughts.

_____

_____

_____

_____

_____

_____

_____

Daily Reflection:

Use the page below to write your feelings or reflections from the chapter or take this time to write out your action plan to begin Creating Greater Thoughts.

Chapter Two

Anchoring in Gratitude: Harnessing The Power of Positive Thinking

"Embrace the power of positive thinking and witness the transformation it brings. With a mindset of optimism and belief, you unlock endless possibilities and pave your own path to success."

Welcome to Section Two, briefly we'll take a moment to review some key points from Section One. In Section One, you learned about the hypothalamus, a part of your brain, which has a lot to do with your emotions and overall wellbeing. You engaged in various activities, accompanied by affirmations and thought-provoking quotes, challenging your current thinking patterns and helping you become aware of your thoughts. Your environment, including the people you love and the broader culture, has greatly influenced your thinking. Now, in Section Two, our focus will be on correcting and transforming your thoughts. I will continue to challenge you, but I also want you to challenge yourself to think differently. This book will remain a valuable resource for you throughout your journey, and you can also share its knowledge to benefit your children, friends, and family. You may even find yourself discussing your thought-challenging experiences with unexpected individuals.

Remember, you are in control of your desires and thoughts, despite external circumstances. We previously discussed going to the gym as a metaphor for this journey. Just like starting a workout routine, we begin small and gradually build up strength. You wouldn't expect to lift heavy weights right away, but with consistent effort, you'll eventually achieve remarkable results. The same principle applies to correcting your thoughts over the next 30 days. We will start with small steps, incorporating powerful affirmations into your daily routine. The affirmations will emphasize the phrase "I am" because you have the potential to become everything you desire.

Throughout this section, you will continue to engage in activities that span 30 days. As you focus on correcting your thoughts, remember to rely on the affirmations whenever negative or unhelpful thoughts arise. Repeat them to yourself, at least three times a day, and allow them to guide and inspire you. Some may find themselves repeating them even more frequently, while others may need a few reminders throughout the day. Every day won't be equally challenging, but remember to take it one day at a time and remain encouraged. Lift your spirits and feel uplifted because you are capable. Embrace the initial similarity to the previous 30 days as we progress into the second phase.

Now, let's reflect on the ABCs to Z analogy. Just as you learned the alphabet through repeated practice, creating new thoughts will also require muscle memory. At first, it may feel deliberate, but as you continue, it will become second nature. Prepare yourself for the upcoming "My Movement," which will soon become "Your Movement" as we reach day 61. I'm excited to witness the progress you will make. Journaling may have been a new experience for some, while for others, it's already ingrained in their routine. Remember, growth is what we all strive for, and by taking it one day at a time, you're steadily moving forward, leaving stagnation behind.

Your muscles are growing stronger, your energy is increasing, and your enthusiasm is contagious. People are drawn to your positive transformation and wondering how you're achieving it. The answer lies in your elevated thoughts, which surpass those of yesterday. And you're accomplishing this progress one day at a time. Get ready for what lies ahead. Day

31 is approaching, and I look forward to reconnecting with you on day 61.

Day 31

Don't live yesterday, today! Today, Build your Tomorrow!

Weekly Guided Scripture

"For in him all things were created: things in heaven and on earth, visible and invisible, whether thrones or powers or rulers or authorities; all things have been created through him and for him." - **Colossians 1:16 NIV**

Today's Activity:

Write down three things you are grateful for. Reflect on the positive aspects of your life and let gratitude set the tone for your thoughts.

_____

_____

_____

_____

_____

_____

_____

_____

_____

Daily Reflection:

Use the page below to write your feelings or reflections from the chapter or take this time to write out your action plan to begin Creating Greater Thoughts.

Day 32

Love, Peace, Knowledge, Wisdom, and Understanding

I AM!

Weekly Guided Scripture

"For in him all things were created: things in heaven and on earth, visible and invisible, whether thrones or powers or rulers or authorities; all things have been created through him and for him." - **Colossians 1:16 NIV**

Today's Activity:

Practice mindful meditation for ten minutes. Focus on your breathing. Cultivate a sense of calm and clarity in your mind.

_____

_____

_____

_____

_____

_____

_____

_____

_____

_____

Daily Reflection:

Use the page below to write your feelings or reflections from the chapter or take this time to write out your action plan to begin Creating Greater Thoughts.

Day 33
Complacency comes with familiarity!

Upgrade your surroundings.

Weekly Guided Scripture
"For in him all things were created: things in heaven and on earth, visible and invisible, whether thrones or powers or rulers or authorities; all things have been created through him and for him." - **Colossians 1:16 NIV**

Today's Activity:
Compile a list of individuals and locations where familiarity has stifled growth. Assess whether temporarily distancing yourself from them is necessary for personal development.

_____

_____

_____

_____

_____

_____

_____

_____

_____

Daily Reflection:

Use the page below to write your feelings or reflections from the chapter or take this time to write out your action plan to begin Creating Greater Thoughts.

Day 34

My strength comes from the most high, so I am able! My heart's desires, I am achieving! I am living a life of abundance!

Weekly Guided Scripture

"For in him all things were created: things in heaven and on earth, visible and invisible, whether thrones or powers or rulers or authorities; all things have been created through him and for him." - **Colossians 1:16 NIV**

Today's Activity:

Engage in a guided visualization exercise. Visualize yourself achieving your desired goals and experiencing success. Notice how this practice influences your thoughts and emotions.

_____

_____

_____

_____

_____

_____

_____

_____

_____

Daily Reflection:

Use the page below to write your feelings or reflections from the chapter or take this time to write out your action plan to begin Creating Greater Thoughts.

Day 35

Mind, body and spirit, I am balanced! Breath in my body, I am blessed! I have all my desires! I am a believer!

Weekly Guided Scripture

"For in him all things were created: things in heaven and on earth, visible and invisible, whether thrones or powers or rulers or authorities; all things have been created through him and for him." - **Colossians 1:16 NIV**

Today's Activity:

Perform random acts of kindness throughout the day. Engaging in selfless acts nurtures positive thoughts and fosters a sense of connection and well-being.

_____

_____

_____

_____

_____

_____

_____

_____

_____

Daily Reflection:

Use the page below to write your feelings or reflections from the chapter or take this time to write out your action plan to begin Creating Greater Thoughts.

Day 36

I show gratitude daily, I am consistent! I find multiple ways,
I am creative! To all my desires, I am connected!

Weekly Guided Scripture

*"For in him all things were created: things in heaven and on
earth, visible and invisible, whether thrones or powers or rulers
or authorities; all things have been created through him and for
him."* - **Colossians 1:16 NIV**

Today's Activity:

Engage in a creative activity such as painting, writing, or
playing music. Observe how the act of creation influences
your thoughts and state of mind.

_____

_____

_____

_____

_____

_____

_____

_____

_____

Daily Reflection:

Use the page below to write your feelings or reflections from the chapter or take this time to write out your action plan to begin Creating Greater Thoughts.

Day 37

Speaking out of love, I am devoted! Towards my goals, I am diligent! Life of abundance, I am deserving!

Weekly Guided Scripture

"For in him all things were created: things in heaven and on earth, visible and invisible, whether thrones or powers or rulers or authorities; all things have been created through him and for him." - **Colossians 1:16 NIV**

Today's Activity:

Write a letter expressing gratitude to someone who has positively impacted your life. Focus on the positive aspects of your relationship and the gratitude you feel.

_____

_____

_____

_____

_____

_____

_____

_____

_____

Daily Reflection:

Use the page below to write your feelings or reflections from the chapter or take this time to write out your action plan to begin Creating Greater Thoughts.

Day 38

Blessings from God, I am excited! Completions of goals, I am executing! My life is full of joy, I am energized!

Weekly Guided Scripture

"Do not be anxious about anything, but in every situation, by prayer and petition, with thanksgiving, present your requests to God. And the peace of God, which transcends all understanding, will guard your hearts and your minds in Christ Jesus." -
Philippians 4:6-7

Today's Activity:

Practice multiple 30-second breathing exercises throughout the day. (Inhaling for five seconds and exhaling for 5 seconds) Pay attention to the present moment and use each breath as an opportunity to cultivate the emotion of goal completion.

_____

_____

_____

_____

_____

_____

_____

_____

Daily Reflection:

Use the page below to write your feelings or reflections from the chapter or take this time to write out your action plan to begin Creating Greater Thoughts.

Day 39

The wrong I've done, I am forgiven! Unexpected blessings, I am fortunate! Challenges upon me, I am fearless!

Weekly Guided Scripture

"Do not be anxious about anything, but in every situation, by prayer and petition, with thanksgiving, present your requests to God. And the peace of God, which transcends all understanding, will guard your hearts and your minds in Christ Jesus." - **Philippians 4:6-7**

Today's Activity:

Monitor your self-talk throughout the day. Replace any negative or self-limiting thoughts with positive and empowering statements about yourself.

_____

_____

_____

_____

_____

_____

_____

_____

_____

Daily Reflection:

Use the page below to write your feelings or reflections from the chapter or take this time to write out your action plan to begin Creating Greater Thoughts.

Day 40

Built for spiritual war, I am a gladiator! Thought to creation, I am gifted! Living for the now, I am grateful!

Weekly Guided Scripture

"Do not be anxious about anything, but in every situation, by prayer and petition, with thanksgiving, present your requests to God. And the peace of God, which transcends all understanding, will guard your hearts and your minds in Christ Jesus." - **Philippians 4:6-7**

Today's Activity:

Spend some time thinking about something you created that came from a thought you had and how completion made you grateful. Write about the feeling and what it was that you created.

_____

_____

_____

_____

_____

_____

_____

_____

_____

Daily Reflection:

Use the page below to write your feelings or reflections from the chapter or take this time to write out your action plan to begin Creating Greater Thoughts.

Day 41

Sorrow is wiped away, I am happy! Alive another day, I am honored! Blessed in every way, I am humble!

Weekly Guided Scripture

"Do not be anxious about anything, but in every situation, by prayer and petition, with thanksgiving, present your requests to God. And the peace of God, which transcends all understanding, will guard your hearts and your minds in Christ Jesus." - **Philippians 4:6-7**

Today's Activity:

Spend time in nature, immersing yourself in its beauty. Observe all that God has created. Allow it to impact your thoughts, promoting a sense of peace and well-being.

_____

_____

_____

_____

_____

_____

_____

_____

_____

_____

Daily Reflection:

Use the page below to write your feelings or reflections from the chapter or take this time to write out your action plan to begin Creating Greater Thoughts.

Day 42

Negativity in thought, I am immune! Endless possibilities, I
am inspired! Better than yesterday, I am!

Weekly Guided Scripture

*"Do not be anxious about anything, but in every situation, by
prayer and petition, with thanksgiving, present your requests
to God. And the peace of God, which transcends all understanding, will guard your hearts and your minds in Christ
Jesus."* - **Philippians 4:6-7**

Today's Activity:

Engage in a limitless visualization exercise specifically focused on your personal and professional success. See yourself
achieving your goals and feel the positive emotions associated
with it.

_____

_____

_____

_____

_____

_____

_____

_____

_____

Daily Reflection:

Use the page below to write your feelings or reflections from the chapter or take this time to write out your action plan to begin Creating Greater Thoughts.

Day 43

Due to the blood, I am justified! Choices in life, I am judicious! My storehouse is full, I am jubilant!

Weekly Guided Scripture

"Do not be anxious about anything, but in every situation, by prayer and petition, with thanksgiving, present your requests to God. And the peace of God, which transcends all understanding, will guard your hearts and your minds in Christ Jesus." - **Philippians 4:6-7**

Today's Activity:

Take a moment to assess your current mindset. Are there any negative thought patterns that need adjusting? Reframe them with positive alternatives.

_____

_____

_____

_____

_____

_____

_____

_____

_____

Daily Reflection:

Use the page below to write your feelings or reflections from the chapter or take this time to write out your action plan to begin Creating Greater Thoughts.

Day 44

Because I ask, I am kept! Thoughtlessly giving, I am kind! I ascertain the wise, I am kingly!

Weekly Guided Scripture

"Do not be anxious about anything, but in every situation, by prayer and petition, with thanksgiving, present your requests to God. And the peace of God, which transcends all understanding, will guard your hearts and your minds in Christ Jesus." - **Philippians 4:6-7**

Today's Activity:

Reflect on the positive affirmations you have been using. Write down any evidence or experiences that support these affirmations, reinforcing their validity.

_____

_____

_____

_____

_____

_____

_____

_____

_____

Daily Reflection:

Use the page below to write your feelings or reflections from the chapter or take this time to write out your action plan to begin Creating Greater Thoughts.

Day 45

To my higher self, I am listening! More about myself, I am learning! Alive for another day, I am loved!

Weekly Guided Scripture

"If you believe, you will receive whatever you ask for in prayer."-
Matthew 21:22

Today's Activity:

As you move about today, observe the beauty of Life around you. Practice gratitude by expressing appreciation for the sights, sounds, and experiences you encounter.

_____

_____

_____

_____

_____

_____

_____

_____

_____

Daily Reflection:

Use the page below to write your feelings or reflections from the chapter or take this time to write out your action plan to begin Creating Greater Thoughts.

Day 46

Through my thoughts, I am manifesting! Controlled emotion, I am mastering it! Love, health and wealth "I Am" is miraculous!

Weekly Guided Scripture

"If you believe, you will receive whatever you ask for in prayer."- **Matthew 21:22**

Today's Activity:

Dedicate the day to self-care activities that bring you joy and relaxation. Nurture yourself and observe how positive self-care practices impact your thoughts.

_____

_____

_____

_____

_____

_____

_____

_____

_____

Daily Reflection:

Use the page below to write your feelings or reflections from the chapter or take this time to write out your action plan to begin Creating Greater Thoughts.

Day 47

To spread love, I am necessary! Due to grace and mercy, I am new! As for worry and stress, I am nonchalant!

Weekly Guided Scripture

"If you believe, you will receive whatever you ask for in prayer."- **Matthew 21:22**

Today's Activity:

Take time to write down the things that are still seeming to cause you stress. When complete write I will no longer stress over this list. Sign and date it.

_____

_____

_____

_____

_____

_____

_____

_____

_____

Daily Reflection:

Use the page below to write your feelings or reflections from the chapter or take this time to write out your action plan to begin Creating Greater Thoughts.

Day 48

To the unseen situations, I am optimistic! Listening to my higher self, I am obedient! A life beyond belief, I am opulent!

Weekly Guided Scripture

"If you believe, you will receive whatever you ask for in prayer."- **Matthew 21:22**

Today's Activity:

Use social media intentionally to connect with positive communities, inspiring content, and uplifting messages. Engage in discussions that promote positive thinking.

_____

_____

_____

_____

_____

_____

_____

_____

_____

Daily Reflection:

Use the page below to write your feelings or reflections from the chapter or take this time to write out your action plan to begin Creating Greater Thoughts.

Day 49

Generosity is life, I am polite! With my goals in life, I am precise! My thoughts are energy, I am powerful!

Weekly Guided Scripture

"If you believe, you will receive whatever you ask for in prayer."- **Matthew 21:22**

Today's Activity:

Set clear and achievable goals for yourself. Break them down into actionable steps and focus your thoughts on the progress you can make.

_____

_____

_____

_____

_____

_____

_____

_____

_____

_____

Daily Reflection:

Use the page below to write your feelings or reflections from the chapter or take this time to write out your action plan to begin Creating Greater Thoughts.

Day 50

The power of thought, I am not quiet! For the toughest jobs, I am qualified! Calm, classy and strong, I am quintessential!

Weekly Guided Scripture

"If you believe, you will receive whatever you ask for in prayer."- **Matthew 21:22**

Today's Activity:

Practice mindful eating by savoring each bite, paying attention to flavors, and enjoying nourishing food. Notice the strength that comes from eating well and how this mindful practice brings forth clear thoughts.

_____

_____

_____

_____

_____

_____

_____

_____

_____

Daily Reflection:

Use the page below to write your feelings or reflections from the chapter or take this time to write out your action plan to begin Creating Greater Thoughts.

Day 51

Because I was created, I am relevant! A bright shining light, I
am radiant! In my quest for joy I am resilient!

Weekly Guided Scripture

*"If you believe, you will receive whatever you ask for in
prayer."* - **Matthew 21:22**

Today's Activity:

Reflect on the progress you have made in cultivating positive thinking. Celebrate the shifts in your mindset and acknowledge the growth you've achieved.

_____

_____

_____

_____

_____

_____

_____

_____

_____

Daily Reflection:

Use the page below to write your feelings or reflections from the chapter or take this time to write out your action plan to begin Creating Greater Thoughts.

Day 52

Because of his life, I am saved! My mind is renewed, I am sure! tribulations in life, I am superior!

Weekly Guided Scripture

"As the body without the spirit is dead, so faith without deeds is dead." - **James 2:26**

Today's Activity:

Take a break from digital devices for the day. To prepare the mind for the work you are about to do. Disconnecting from screens allows space for positive thoughts and increased presence in the moment.

_____

_____

_____

_____

_____

_____

_____

_____

_____

Daily Reflection:

Use the page below to write your feelings or reflections from the chapter or take this time to write out your action plan to begin Creating Greater Thoughts.

Day 53

Overcoming the stress, I am triumphant! Only the positive, I am thinking! Abundant above belief, I am thankful!

Weekly Guided Scripture

"As the body without the spirit is dead, so faith without deeds is dead." - **James 2:26**

Today's Activity:

Practice self-compassion by speaking triumphantly to yourself and treating yourself with understanding and forgiveness. Notice how this practice shapes your thoughts and self-perception.

_____

_____

_____

_____

_____

_____

_____

_____

_____

Daily Reflection:

Use the page below to write your feelings or reflections from the chapter or take this time to write out your action plan to begin Creating Greater Thoughts.

Day 54

Trust in the Most High, I am unwavering! To God the creator of the universe, I am unified! Another day of life, I am uplifted!

Weekly Guided Scripture

"As the body without the spirit is dead, so faith without deeds is dead." - **James 2:26**

Today's Activity:

Since starting this journey, what were you hopeful for that you have already achieved and how has that made you feel?

_____

_____

_____

_____

_____

_____

_____

_____

_____

Daily Reflection:

Use the page below to write your feelings or reflections from the chapter or take this time to write out your action plan to begin Creating Greater Thoughts.

Day 55

Against all challenges, I am valiant! More than enough, I am
vigorous! Thoughts of a winner, I am victorious!

Weekly Guided Scripture

*"As the body without the spirit is dead, so faith without deeds is
dead."* - **James 2:26**

Today's Activity:

Dedicate time to journaling about victories. Write about
the things, experiences, and people you are grateful for during
the battle to success. Notice the impact on your feelings and
overall well-being.

_____

_____

_____

_____

_____

_____

_____

_____

_____

Daily Reflection:

Use the page below to write your feelings or reflections from the chapter or take this time to write out your action plan to begin Creating Greater Thoughts.

Day 56

My gratitude speaks, I am winning! My 3rd eye is active, I am wired! Living out my dreams, I am worthy!

Weekly Guided Scripture

"As the body without the spirit is dead, so faith without deeds is dead." - **James 2:26**

Today's Activity:

Consciously choose positive and uplifting media to consume for the day. Whether it's books, movies or podcasts, immerse yourself in content that inspires and uplifts your thoughts.

_____

_____

_____

_____

_____

_____

_____

_____

_____

Daily Reflection:

Use the page below to write your feelings or reflections from the chapter or take this time to write out your action plan to begin Creating Greater Thoughts.

Day 57

Using my life to bless, I am xenodochial! To negative nonsense, I am x-ray vision, A lifted mind state, I am a xenagogue!

Weekly Guided Scripture

"As the body without the spirit is dead, so faith without deeds is dead." - **James 2:26**

Today's Activity:

A xenagogue is a guide. Take time today to guide to someone you see or know is in need of a mental state uplift. How did it feel to be the one to help them?

_____

_____

_____

_____

_____

_____

_____

_____

_____

Daily Reflection:

Use the page below to write your feelings or reflections from the chapter or take this time to write out your action plan to begin Creating Greater Thoughts.

Day 58

To the Most High, I am yielding! Imagining many ways, I am
yeasty! Wealthy and healthy, I am you!

Weekly Guided Scripture

*"As the body without the spirit is dead, so faith without deeds is
dead."* - **James 2:26**

Today's Activity:

Remember it's not how but who. Write a list of who you
know who can help you reach your health and wealth goals.
Ask them to guide you. Take notes on their advice.

_____

_____

_____

_____

_____

_____

_____

_____

_____

Daily Reflection:

Use the page below to write your feelings or reflections from the chapter or take this time to write out your action plan to begin Creating Greater Thoughts.

Day 59

Due to the Trinity, I am zestful! About my desires, I am zealous! Because I have, I am zippy

Weekly Guided Scripture

"As the body without the spirit is dead, so faith without deeds is dead." - **James 2:26**

Today's Activity:

Engage in an activity that allows you to release emotions, such as journaling, dancing, or talking with a trusted friend. Observe the impact only our thoughts and mental clarity.

_____

_____

_____

_____

_____

_____

_____

Daily Reflection:

Use the page below to write your feelings or reflections from the chapter or take this time to write out your action plan to begin Creating Greater Thoughts.

Day 60
"I am" the answer, to my desires

Weekly Guided Scripture

"As the body without the spirit is dead, so faith without deeds is dead." - **James 2:26**

Today's Activity:

Write down three positive views of yourself that currently reside within you that you didn't believe when you started this journey.

_____

_____

_____

_____

_____

_____

_____

Daily Reflection:

Use the page below to write your feelings or reflections from the chapter or take this time to write out your action plan to begin Creating Greater Thoughts.

Chapter Three

Seeds of Transformation: Planting The Seeds of Empowering Thoughts

"Plant the seeds of empowering thoughts in the garden of your mind, and watch them bloom into a flourishing forest of limitless potential. Nourish them with belief, cultivate them with perseverance, and witness the harvest of a life filled with purpose and achievement."

G reat job! I'm immensely proud of you. Today marks your 61st day, and we are progressing steadily. Your muscles have started to grow, and your muscle memory is beginning to take full effect. You are now becoming aware of thoughts that no longer serve you well. You're recognizing the reactions you used to have, how they would snowball into a negative spiral, even escalating into an avalanche. But those days are over. Do you still experience those negative avalanches? If so, that's normal, so don't beat yourself. If this sounds like you and you're still experiencing those negative avalanches, acknowledge them, affirm yourself, and move forward remembering how far you've already come. Now, you're shifting towards avalanches of positivity. Each wave of positivity multiplies, forming a powerful tsunami.

I'm proud of you, and you should be proud of yourself too. You've reached the age of 61 days, and soon you'll complete 90 days. On that day, you will have made it. Your muscles will have fully developed. When you look in the mirror, you'll love the person staring back at you. You'll be able to say it out loud, directly to yourself. Embrace your growth and get excited about it. At this point, we are consciously aware of our thoughts. We've corrected them and cultivated excitement. Now, we will move forward to recreate our thoughts using a technique I mentioned earlier: "My Movement."

Before delving into "My Movement," which will soon be referred to as "Your Movement," let's revisit day 60. You said, "I am the answer to my desires." Remember, it is you who's doing the work. You are the one lifting the weight, allowing your mind to grow and expand. You are not limited by others, as all the resources needed are already within your reach. The world has been created this way by God, who designed it for free spirits like you. Embrace your identity as the answer to your desires and let's fulfill them. Let's fight the good fight for ourselves. Now, as we explore the "My movement," remember to meditate on it because it will be immensely helpful. I'm thrilled to share with you your next activity.

In this final segment, I will introduce you to "My Movement," also known as the Greater Vest, representing the power of greater thoughts. Let me break it down for you. The G stands for gratitude, the V stands for visualization, the E stands for emotions, the S stands for speech, and the T stands for thoughts. In this section, we will explore how to incorporate these elements into our practice.

Let's start with **gratitude**. Expressing gratitude through actions and words is a powerful way to show appreciation for what you already have and what you desire. Remember, you are already connected to your desires. Next is **visualization**. With both open and closed eyes, take the time to vividly imagine and see exactly what you want. Paint a clear picture in your mind, knowing that it is already yours because you are connected to it.

Moving on to **emotions**. Fully immerse yourself in the emotion of already having the desires of your heart. Walk, live, and feel as if you have already achieved what you desire. Don't doubt or dismiss it just because you can't see it yet in the physical.

Now, let's focus on **speech**. Your words have immense

power. Proverbs 18:21 reminds us that death and life are in the power of the tongue. Speak life into what you desire and avoid speaking life into things that should no longer have a place in your life. Be mindful of the importance of your speech throughout this process.

Finally, **thoughts**. Maintain a winning mindset about your desires. Do not allow limitations to trap you. Remember that we are limitless beings, and you have unlimited potential. Embrace expansive and empowering thoughts.

So as we move forward, our focus will remain on the next 30 days of affirmations. These affirmations will challenge you to say things that may have seemed impossible or unrealizable in the past. But with faith, all things are possible. Believe in yourself because you carry the essence of God within you. I want to take a moment to express how proud I am of you for reaching day 60, and I look forward to what awaits us on day 90. Take your time and embrace each day. Remember, it's a journey one day at a time. Keep the excitement alive because it brings joy and positivity to your experience.

During this process, uplift yourself because there may not always be someone there to uplift you. Trials and tribulations come to us all, but what matters is how you handle them, how you treat others during those times, and how you treat yourself. Day 61 is here. Let's prepare ourselves to make it happen and continue this transformative journey.

Day 61

You must enter a new thought process to enter a new life!

Weekly Guided Scripture

"fear not, for I am with you;
be not dismayed, for I am your God;
I will strengthen you, I will help you,
I will uphold you with my righteous right hand."
- Isaiah 41:10

Today's Activity:

Spend a portion of the day in silence and solitude. Allow your thoughts to flow freely and observe their nature without judgement.

_____

_____

_____

_____

_____

_____

_____

Daily Reflection:

Use the page below to write your feelings or reflections from the chapter or take this time to write out your action plan to begin Creating Greater Thoughts.

Day 62

I am grateful! I am loving! I am abundant! I am powerful! I am wealthy! I am confident! I am healthy! I am balanced! I am peaceful! I am openly receiving!

Weekly Guided Scripture

"fear not, for I am with you;
be not dismayed, for I am your God;
I will strengthen you, I will help you,
I will uphold you with my righteous right hand."
- Isaiah 41:10

Today's Activity:

Take a break from social media and digital distractions. Use this time to connect with nature, reflect on your aspirations, and nurture self-care.

_____

_____

_____

_____

_____

_____

_____

Daily Reflection:

Use the page below to write your feelings or reflections from the chapter or take this time to write out your action plan to begin Creating Greater Thoughts.

Day 63

I am connected to infinite Wisdom! I am connected to infinite knowledge! I am Connected to infinite Energy! I am believing in the power of my thoughts! I am filled with enthusiasm about today! I am creating my desires now! I am awake and enlightened! I am in alignment with my goals! I am grateful for the spirit within me! I am hopeful for the future!

Weekly Guided Scripture

"fear not, for I am with you;
be not dismayed, for I am your God;
I will strengthen you, I will help you,
I will uphold you with my righteous right hand."
- Isaiah 41:10

Today's Activity:

Write a letter of appreciation to yourself, acknowledging your strengths, accomplishments, and inner beauty. Read it aloud with self-compassion.

_____

_____

_____

_____

_____

_____

Daily Reflection:

Use the page below to write your feelings or reflections from the chapter or take this time to write out your action plan to begin Creating Greater Thoughts.

Day 64

I am filled with bliss and the energy it creates! I am Pleased with Today! I am not Complacent! I am doing the work now for later success! I am emotionally tied to a positive future! I am loving the outlook of my life! I am consistently receiving good from unexpected people and places, I am moving toward my goals!

Weekly Guided Scripture

"fear not, for I am with you;
be not dismayed, for I am your God;
I will strengthen you, I will help you,
I will uphold you with my righteous right hand."
- Isaiah 41:10

Today's Activity:

Connect with a supportive friend or mentor who uplifts and encourages you. Share your aspirations and receive their words of affirmation and guidance.

_____

_____

_____

_____

_____

_____

Daily Reflection:

Use the page below to write your feelings or reflections from the chapter or take this time to write out your action plan to begin Creating Greater Thoughts.

Day 65

Grateful is what I am! I am filled with the spirit of God! I am winning! I am a leader! I am blessed! I am abundant in all aspects of my life! I am full of joy! I am openly receiving and happily sharing! I am renewed in my mind! Energized is what I am!

Weekly Guided Scripture

"fear not, for I am with you;
be not dismayed, for I am your God;
I will strengthen you, I will help you,
I will uphold you with my righteous right hand."
- Isaiah 41:10

Today's Activity:

Engage in a random act of kindness. Offer assistance, a compliment, or a small gesture of love to someone, and notice how it cultivates positive thoughts within you.

_____

_____

_____

_____

_____

_____

Daily Reflection:

Use the page below to write your feelings or reflections from the chapter or take this time to write out your action plan to begin Creating Greater Thoughts.

Day 66

I am the activator of my mind! I am the change I desire to see! I realize I must expand my comfort zone! I am winning now! I am speaking positivity into my life! I am removing all negative influences! I am an overachiever! I am loving my life of abundance! I am not living a life of lack in any area! I am grateful for the life I live!

Weekly Guided Scripture

"fear not, for I am with you;
be not dismayed, for I am your God;
I will strengthen you, I will help you,
I will uphold you with my righteous right hand."
- Isaiah 41:10

Today's Activity:

Dedicate 15 minutes to visualize your desired future. Envision yourself achieving your goals, feeling empowered, and radiating confidence.

_____

_____

_____

_____

_____

_____

Daily Reflection:

Use the page below to write your feelings or reflections from the chapter or take this time to write out your action plan to begin Creating Greater Thoughts.

Day 67

I am thankful my spirit is connected to the Creator! I am blessed coming and going! I am believing the goodness of God is at work in my life! I am visualizing my desires until they are reality! I am thankful for the past! I am overjoyed with the present and hopeful for tomorrow! I am loving my life! I am a positive light of energy for others to see! I am already healthy, wealthy and abundant!

Weekly Guided Scripture

"fear not, for I am with you;
be not dismayed, for I am your God;
I will strengthen you, I will help you,
I will uphold you with my righteous right hand."
- Isaiah 41:10

Today's Activity:

Practice positive self-talk throughout the day. Replace self-criticism with self-encouragement and remind yourself of your worth and potential.

_____

_____

_____

_____

_____

Daily Reflection:

Use the page below to write your feelings or reflections from the chapter or take this time to write out your action plan to begin Creating Greater Thoughts.

Day 68

Thank you God for the gift of the present! I am free of the concerns of yesterday! I am a winner of today! I am blessed with love! I am a true believer in my positive thoughts! I am receiving the good of the Universe! I show gratitude today for the blessings of tomorrow! This is the truth that I am living! I am already wealthy, healthy and abundant!

Weekly Guided Scripture

"What has been will be again,
what has been done will be done again;
there is nothing new under the sun." - **Ecclesiastes 1:9 NIV**

Today's Activity:

Explore a new hobby or skill that you've been curious about. Embrace the learning process and celebrate your progress along the way.

_____

_____

_____

_____

_____

_____

Daily Reflection:

Use the page below to write your feelings or reflections from the chapter or take this time to write out your action plan to begin Creating Greater Thoughts.

Day 69

My thoughts are filled with gratefulness! I am filled with positive energy! I am blessed by the spirit of love! My life is moving toward all I desire! I am thankful for receiving above my goals! I am vibrating at a high level and attracting others like myself! I am enjoying the life I live! I believe that God through the universe has more for me that I can see! These are the words of faith which I speak, I am already Healthy, Wealthy, and Abundant!

Weekly Guided Scripture

"What has been will be again,
what has been done will be done again;
there is nothing new under the sun." - **Ecclesiastes 1:9 NIV**

Today's Activity:

Engage in an open hearted activity. Write, email, or text a heartfelt letter to someone you appreciate.

_____

_____

_____

_____

_____

Daily Reflection:

Use the page below to write your feelings or reflections from the chapter or take this time to write out your action plan to begin Creating Greater Thoughts.

Day 70

I am grateful for my God given gifts! I am confident! I am a leader in all I do! I know I am worthy of my desires! I am working towards my goals daily! I am speaking life into my situations! I am successful in all areas of my life! I am filled with good energy! I am creating opportunities through my gifts! I am blessed beyond words!

Weekly Guided Scripture

"What has been will be again,
what has been done will be done again;
there is nothing new under the sun." - **Ecclesiastes 1:9 NIV**

Today's Activity:

Create a vision board, size it up to you. Cut out images and words that represent your aspirations and goals. Display it in a prominent place (where you can see it daily) as a visual reminder of your dreams.

_____

_____

_____

_____

_____

_____

_____

Daily Reflection:

Use the page below to write your feelings or reflections from the chapter or take this time to write out your action plan to begin Creating Greater Thoughts.

Day 71

I am never in lack! I am filled with joy today! I am thankful for seeing eyes! I am grateful for working lungs! I am excited for today's experiences! I am receiving from God's abundance! I am increasing in positive energy now! I am using my thoughts to create change! I am spreading love to everyone I contact!

Weekly Guided Scripture

"What has been will be again,
what has been done will be done again;
there is nothing new under the sun." - **Ecclesiastes 1:9 NIV**

Today's Activity:

Take the day to notice all the ways you are receiving Gods overflow in your life.

_____

_____

_____

_____

_____

_____

_____

Daily Reflection:

Use the page below to write your feelings or reflections from the chapter or take this time to write out your action plan to begin Creating Greater Thoughts.

Day 72

I am enlightened by the most high! I am excited for the
blessings of today! I am filled with love! My thoughts are
focused on positivity! Negative thoughts have no place in my
mind! I am at the right place at the right time, my timing is
impeccable! I am the energy created by my thoughts! I am
evidence that high vibration leads to joy! I am already healthy,
wealthy and abundant!

Weekly Guided Scripture

"What has been will be again,
what has been done will be done again;
there is nothing new under the sun." - **Ecclesiastes 1:9 NIV**

Today's Activity:

Write down any self-limiting beliefs that arise throughout
the day. Challenge them by reframing them into positive,
empowering statements.

_____

_____

_____

_____

_____

_____

_____

Daily Reflection:

Use the page below to write your feelings or reflections from the chapter or take this time to write out your action plan to begin Creating Greater Thoughts.

Day 73

I am directly connected to the spirit of the most high! My desires are happening in my life today! I am not leaning on my own understanding! I am allowing my higher self to work for me! I am visualizing how joy and happiness looks to me! My thoughts create my energy to create now! I am not allowing my ego to disrupt my success! I am filled with gratitude! My mind is renewed and positivity flows! I think highly of myself!

Weekly Guided Scripture

"What has been will be again,
what has been done will be done again;
there is nothing new under the sun." - **Ecclesiastes 1:9 NIV**

Today's Activity:

Use social media today to follow new accounts such as podcasts, or blogs that share empowering messages and stories of personal growth.

_____

_____

_____

_____

_____

_____

Daily Reflection:

Use the page below to write your feelings or reflections from the chapter or take this time to write out your action plan to begin Creating Greater Thoughts.

Day 74

I am strengthened by love! I am making the correct decisions! I am experiencing good things daily! I am filled with courage! I am worthy! I am a resonator of high vibrations! I am creating through my positive thoughts! I am energized by the endless possibilities to have all I desire! I am blessed by the holy I am!

Weekly Guided Scripture

"What has been will be again,
what has been done will be done again;
there is nothing new under the sun." - **Ecclesiastes 1:9 NIV**

Today's Activity:

Take a technology detox day. Disconnect from screens and engage in activities that nourish your mind, body, and soul, such as reading, journaling, or spending time in nature.

_____

_____

_____

_____

_____

_____

_____

Daily Reflection:

Use the page below to write your feelings or reflections from the chapter or take this time to write out your action plan to begin Creating Greater Thoughts.

Day 75

I am created from the love of God! I am thankful for waking another day! I am elated because I have already won! I am grateful the universe has all I need! I am aligned with my desires! I am achieving all my goals! I am living the life of abundance! I am emitting high vibrations! I am living a life of joy!

Weekly Guided Scripture

"Jesus looked at them and said, "With man this is impossible, but with God all things are possible." - **Matthew 19:26 NIV**

Today's Activity:

Explore a new genre of music that inspires and uplifts you. Create a playlist of empowering songs and listen to it throughout the day.

_____

_____

_____

_____

_____

_____

Daily Reflection:

Use the page below to write your feelings or reflections from the chapter or take this time to write out your action plan to begin Creating Greater Thoughts.

Day 76

I am thankful for the flesh! I am emotionally High and Shining bright! I am a Joyous being! I am a forgiving Person! I am connected though the spirit! I am excited for the Day!

Weekly Guided Scripture

"Jesus looked at them and said, "With man this is impossible, but with God all things are possible." - **Matthew 19:26 NIV**

Today's Activity:

Practice forgiveness. Release any resentments or grudges you may be holding, and affirm your willingness to let go and cultivate inner peace.

_____

_____

_____

_____

_____

_____

Daily Reflection:

Use the page below to write your feelings or reflections from the chapter or take this time to write out your action plan to begin Creating Greater Thoughts.

Day 77

I am showing gratitude by being loving! I am worthy of the blessing I receive! I am living out my dreams! I am successful in all I do! I am making the best decision first! I am positive and excited about my future! I am healthy in Mind, Body, and Spirit!

Weekly Guided Scripture

"Jesus looked at them and said, "With man this is impossible, but with God all things are possible." - **Matthew 19:26 NIV**

Today's Activity:

Write a love letter to your body, expressing gratitude for its strength, resilience, and beauty. Embrace self-acceptance and nurture a positive body image.

_____

_____

_____

_____

_____

_____

_____

Daily Reflection:

Use the page below to write your feelings or reflections from the chapter or take this time to write out your action plan to begin Creating Greater Thoughts.

Day 78

I am filled with gratitude for my life! I am living with purpose today! I am choosing to place my focus on positivity! I am creating high vibrations! I am radiating from the joys of life! I am a bright light and my actions are aligned! I am spreading love through my voice! I am excited for new experiences! I am receiving goods from everywhere! I am encouraged!

Weekly Guided Scripture

"Jesus looked at them and said, "With man this is impossible, but with God all things are possible." - **Matthew 19:26 NIV**

Today's Activity:

Engage in a creative activity that allows you to express yourself, such as painting, writing, or crafting. Embrace the joy of creation and let your imagination soar.

_____

_____

_____

_____

_____

_____

Daily Reflection:

Use the page below to write your feelings or reflections from the chapter or take this time to write out your action plan to begin Creating Greater Thoughts.

Day 79

I am open minded with a renewed spirit! I am always at the right place at the right time! I speak positive words into the lives of others because I love myself! I am thankful for my unique gifts and using my gifts to bless others! I am the controller of my thoughts and they stay positive! I am enlightened by the holy I am and I am staying in alignment to receive the good God has for me!

Weekly Guided Scripture

"Jesus looked at them and said, "With man this is impossible, but with God all things are possible." - **Matthew 19:26 NIV**

Today's Activity:

Engage in a digital decluttering session. Unsubscribe from negative or triggering content and curate your digital spaces to align with your empowering thoughts. Journal about the new emotions.

_____

_____

_____

_____

Daily Reflection:

Use the page below to write your feelings or reflections from the chapter or take this time to write out your action plan to begin Creating Greater Thoughts.

Day 80

I am wealthy because I have life! I am a beacon of light! I am shining bright! I am spreading love! I am attracting all positive things to my life! My thoughts allow me to create greatness!

Weekly Guided Scripture

"Jesus looked at them and said, "With man this is impossible, but with God all things are possible." - **Matthew 19:26 NIV**

Today's Activity:

Practice acts of self-care that nurture your mind, body, and spirit. Take a long bath, indulge in a nourishing meal, or engage in activities that bring you joy.

_____

_____

_____

_____

_____

_____

_____

Daily Reflection:

Use the page below to write your feelings or reflections from the chapter or take this time to write out your action plan to begin Creating Greater Thoughts.

Day 81

I am excited for the goodness of today! I am enjoying the life I desire! I am moving towards my dreams daily! I am never weak, better yet, I am strong! I am blessed by the Universe's abundance! I am connected to God who provides all! I am thankful for my health! I am wealthy! I am living a life of joy!

Weekly Guided Scripture

"Jesus looked at them and said, "With man this is impossible, but with God all things are possible." - **Matthew 19:26 NIV**

Today's Activity:

Practice a loving-kindness meditation. Send wishes of love, compassion, and well-being to yourself and to all beings around the world.

_____

_____

_____

_____

_____

_____

Daily Reflection:

Use the page below to write your feelings or reflections from the chapter or take this time to write out your action plan to begin Creating Greater Thoughts.

Day 82

I am blessed though the spirit! I am at peace today! I am Freed of negative thoughts! I am speaking the truth I desire! I am creating by way of a renewed mind! I am focused on feeding my mind positivity! I am refraining from the confusion of the world! I am feeling Loved and Prosperous! I am faithful to the Holy I Am!

Weekly Guided Scripture

"Jesus looked at them and said, "With man this is impossible, but with God all things are possible." - **Matthew 19:26 NIV**

Today's Activity:

Create a positive mantra that aligns with your goals and aspirations. Repeat it throughout the day, allowing it to anchor empowering thoughts in your mind.

_____

_____

_____

_____

_____

_____

Daily Reflection:

Use the page below to write your feelings or reflections from the chapter or take this time to write out your action plan to begin Creating Greater Thoughts.

Day 83

I am grateful to see another day! I am using the trials in my life to fuel my growth! I am excited for the blessings of tomorrow! I am deserving of the gifts of the most high! I am and thankful and loved! I am focused on the positive outcomes in my life! I am happy for others when they achieve! I have faith the desires of my heart are mine! I believe in myself! I am a renewed mind!

Weekly Guided Scripture

"Now to him who is able to do immeasurably more than all we ask or imagine, according to his power that is at work within us, 21. to him be glory in the church and in Christ Jesus throughout all generations, for ever and ever! Amen." - **Ephesians 3:20–21 NIV**

Today's Activity:

Take time today to take notice when others achieve a goal or do well in a specific situation. Praise them aloud and pay close attention to the positive effect it has on your mood and mindset.

_____

_____

_____

_____

Daily Reflection:

Use the page below to write your feelings or reflections from the chapter or take this time to write out your action plan to begin Creating Greater Thoughts.

Day 84

I am Thankful for life! I am blessed today! I am abundant! I am loving my life! I am grateful for all I have! I am using my gifts to bless others! I am openly receiving what God has for me! I am a believer in myself.

Weekly Guided Scripture

"Now to him who is able to do immeasurably more than all we ask or imagine, according to his power that is at work within us, 21. to him be glory in the church and in Christ Jesus throughout all generations, for ever and ever! Amen." - **Ephesians 3:20–21 NIV**

Today's Activity:

Write down three recent achievements or milestones, no matter how small. Celebrate them and acknowledge your growth and progress.

_____

_____

_____

_____

_____

_____

Daily Reflection:

Use the page below to write your feelings or reflections from the chapter or take this time to write out your action plan to begin Creating Greater Thoughts.

Day 85

I am the activator of my mind! I am the change I desire to see! I realize I must expand my comfort zone! I am winning now! I am speaking positivity into my life! I and a remover of negative influences! I am an overachiever! I am loving my life of abundance! I am not living a life of lack in any area! I am grateful for the life I live!

Weekly Guided Scripture

"Now to him who is able to do immeasurably more than all we ask or imagine, according to his power that is at work within us, 21. to him be glory in the church and in Christ Jesus throughout all generations, for ever and ever! Amen." - **Ephesians 3:20–21 NIV**

Today's Activity:

Reflect on the lessons and growth you've experienced in the past 24 days. Write a letter to yourself, expressing how affirmation has helped you grow.

_____

_____

_____

_____

_____

_____

Daily Reflection:

Use the page below to write your feelings or reflections from the chapter or take this time to write out your action plan to begin Creating Greater Thoughts.

Day 86

I am blessed to see another day! I am the sole controller of my thoughts! My emotions are in alignment with my thoughts and with my positive energy! I am not allowing negative people to change my positive attitude! I am thankful for the life I have! I am using my gifts to bless others! I am already wealthy, healthy and abundant!

Weekly Guided Scripture

"Now to him who is able to do immeasurably more than all we ask or imagine, according to his power that is at work within us, 21. to him be glory in the church and in Christ Jesus throughout all generations, for ever and ever! Amen." - **Ephesians 3:20–21 NIV**

Today's Activity:

Practice self-reflection through journaling. Explore your thoughts, feelings and desires. Identify how they cause your emotions to move. Do you feel empowered or defeated? Why?

_____

_____

_____

_____

_____

Daily Reflection:

Use the page below to write your feelings or reflections from the chapter or take this time to write out your action plan to begin Creating Greater Thoughts.

Day 87

When I dream, I believe I am in reality! In reality I smile and feel good, because my dreams are becoming my reality!

Weekly Guided Scripture

"Now to him who is able to do immeasurably more than all we ask or imagine, according to his power that is at work within us, 21. to him be glory in the church and in Christ Jesus throughout all generations, for ever and ever! Amen." - **Ephesians 3:20–21 NIV**

Today's Activity:

Reflect on the journey of harnessing positive thinking. Renew your commitment to maintaining a positive mindset and identify areas for further growth. Remembering there is more than one way to completion.

Daily Reflection:

Use the page below to write your feelings or reflections from the chapter or take this time to write out your action plan to begin Creating Greater Thoughts.

Day 88

I speak that I can & I am! I am grateful for the breath in my Lungs! I am glad that the universe has all that I need! I am worthy of my Blessing! I am Believing that all things are possible for me! My dreams are becoming my reality daily!

Weekly Guided Scripture

"Now to him who is able to do immeasurably more than all we ask or imagine, according to his power that is at work within us, 21. to him be glory in the church and in Christ Jesus throughout all generations, for ever and ever! Amen." - **Ephesians 3:20–21 NIV**

Today's Activity:

Connect with nature and embrace its beauty and serenity. Spend time outdoors, take a walk in a park, or simply sit and observe the natural world around you. Take mental note how all that has been created has come from what the earth provides.

_____

_____

_____

_____

_____

_____

Daily Reflection:

Use the page below to write your feelings or reflections from the chapter or take this time to write out your action plan to begin Creating Greater Thoughts.

Day 89

I am believing in myself! I am loving! I am forgiving! I am
fearless! I am having fun! I am enjoying this life I live! I will
continue on this journey to a new outlook on my life and
grow like a seed planted in good soil next to a vibrant stream!

Weekly Guided Scripture

*"Now to him who is able to do immeasurably more than all we
ask or imagine, according to his power that is at work within us, 21. to him be glory in the church and in Christ Jesus
throughout all generations, for ever and ever! Amen."* - **Ephesians 3:20–21 NIV**

Today's Activity:

Identify one fear or limiting belief that you are ready to
release. Write it down, then tear up the paper symbolizing
your willingness to let it go.

_____

_____

_____

_____

_____

_____

Daily Reflection:

Use the page below to write your feelings or reflections from the chapter or take this time to write out your action plan to begin Creating Greater Thoughts.

Day 90

I celebrate completing my 90-day self-transformation journey! I am a radiant being of limitless potential, embracing my authenticity and embodying divine love! I attract abundance, joy, and meaningful connections! With gratitude, I continue to grow, guided by divine wisdom! I am a vessel of light, walking with grace, purpose, and power! I am grateful for the miracles of the past 90 days and embrace my limitless potential! So it is. Amen.

Weekly Guided Scripture

"Now to him who is able to do immeasurably more than all we ask or imagine, according to his power that is at work within us, 21. to him be glory in the church and in Christ Jesus throughout all generations, for ever and ever! Amen." - **Ephesians 3:20–21 NIV**

Today's Activity:

Create a personal mantra or affirmation that encapsulates your journey of self-transformation and empowers you for the future. Write it down and place it somewhere meaningful and visible, such as on your bedside table or in your wallet. Repeat this mantra daily, allowing it to reinforce your positive mindset and guide your actions moving forward.

_____

_____

_____

_____

_____

_____

Daily Reflection:

Use the page below to write your feelings or reflections from the chapter or take this time to write out your action plan to begin Creating Greater Thoughts.

Living an Empowered Life

As we conclude Greater Thoughts, we reflect upon the transformative journey you have embarked upon—a journey to unlock the hidden potential of your mind. Throughout these pages, we have delved into the intricate workings of the mind and explored the profound impact of our thoughts and energy.

The mind operates as a vessel of energy, constantly influenced by the thoughts we cultivate. Repetition plays a pivotal role in shaping our mental landscape, as cells within our brain reproduce based on the energy we feed them. By understanding this fundamental process, we have unveiled the power to shape our reality through intentional thinking.

However, we have also acknowledged the external factors that have hindered our progress. From early on, society, well-meaning individuals, and limiting beliefs have attempted to confine us within narrow boundaries. But let us remember that these limitations do not define us. They are not our true essence. It is time to break free from the chains that have held us back and reclaim our limitless potential.

Over the course of the last 90 days, we have set forth on a mission to retrain our thought processes. By consistently nurturing positive thoughts and allowing them to reproduce within our minds, we have paved the way for a brighter, more fulfilling future. Each day is an opportunity for growth, a chance to renew our commitment to positivity and self-transformation.

As we have persevered through trials and tribulations, we have witnessed the emergence of a new mindset—a mindset rooted in resilience, empowerment, and unwavering belief in our abilities and trust in God . We have learned to navigate the ebb and flow of negative thoughts, acknowledging their presence but refusing to be entangled in their grip. We have harnessed the power of repetition, making positive thinking a habit that propels us forward.

Now, armed with the tools "GREATER V.E.S.T." and wisdom acquired throughout this journey, it is time to venture forth into the vast expanse of our lives. Let us carry this newfound understanding with us, allowing it to guide our decisions, actions, and interactions with the world. And should we ever find ourselves veering off course, we need only return to these words, to this book, and start afresh.

Remember, our transformation is not confined to ourselves alone. We possess the ability to ignite change in others—our friends, our family, and even future generations. Let us share the knowledge we have gained, spreading the light of possibility and liberation to all those we encounter. Together, we can untrap the minds of everyone we know, nurturing a world where limitless potential reigns supreme.

I want to express my gratitude to you for embarking on this journey of self-discovery and growth. Your dedication and perseverance have been remarkable. I believe in you, and I am confident that you will continue to cultivate positive thoughts, create your own reality, and manifest a life of purpose and fulfillment.

Thank you for being part of this transformative experience. I wish you all the love, success, and joy that life has to offer. Take care of yourself, and may your journey be forever illuminated by the power of the Great and Holy "I Am" within you!

Acknowledgements

I would like to express my deepest gratitude to the remarkable individuals who have influenced and supported me throughout my journey. Their unwavering belief in my potential and their unwavering encouragement during both moments of triumph and adversity have profoundly shaped the path I have taken.

First and foremost, my heartfelt thanks go to my parents, whose constant belief in me has been an unwavering pillar of strength throughout my life. Their enduring support and unwavering faith have been instrumental in my growth and development.

I am also immensely grateful to my younger sister and brother for embracing the transformative power of positive thinking alongside me. Your openness and willingness to adopt this mindset have been invaluable, and I am honored to have shared this journey with you.

A special mention must be made to my dear friend Dre B., who ignited my path to overcoming my limiting beliefs about six years ago. Initially unaware of the constraints within my own mind, Dre B. challenged me to change my way of thinking, leading me to the creation of this book. I am forever grateful for his influence and guidance.

To my incredible children, lovingly referred to as the S.T.A.R., I hope that the lessons I have imparted upon you remain deeply ingrained. As your father, I have strived to teach you how to break free from the limitations imposed by others and to have unwavering faith in your own abilities. I encourage you to revisit this book and share its teachings with others, spreading the message that they too can achieve greatness by following the process and embracing the "Greater V.E.S.T."

I would like to dedicate a special mention to my late friend, John H. Simpson. When I shared my thoughts with him, he eagerly absorbed the concepts and urged me to share them with the world. His constant encouragement and insistence that I teach this philosophy in a classroom setting have deeply resonated within me. John, I am honored to fulfill your vision and carry your spirit forward.

To my unwavering source of support, my beloved Andrea, words fail to capture the immense gratitude I feel for having you in my life. Your unwavering love and support have been my rock, and I consider myself eternally blessed to have you by my side. With you, I have found a true partner, and together we embrace the journey bestowed upon us by a higher power.

God has truly blessed me with 1.L.T.

Finally, my hope is that this book serves as a guiding resource to help you maintain a positive outlook in the face of adversity. May it remind you that all situations, no matter how challenging, are temporary.

About the Author

Get to Know Robert Collins

Robert Collins is a father, husband and community advocate committed to using words to help shape the lives of people, by helping them to understand how God sees them. As a professional committed to seeing the growth of young men and women, Collins uses affirmations and the teachings of scripture to empower readers.

He wants readers to understand the power of character and positive thought, as well as having them understand that one can only rise, conquer and achieve by first elevating their thoughts. For more information about Robert Collins email him at robert@theuntrappedmind.com

Connect With Robert Collins

Instagram: @Greater7Thoughts

Email: robert@theuntrappedmind.com

We'd love to connect with you and talk more about how we can get Greater Thoughts: The Un-Trapped Mind into the hands of people inside your community. Robert would love the opportunity to chat with you on opportunities to speak, conduct workshops or even plan a connection day with your team. For more information email robert@theuntrappedmind.com

* 9 7 9 8 9 8 7 7 1 0 9 6 8 *